When You Were Born in Vietnam

A memory book for children adopted from Vietnam

by **Therese Bartlett** with Photographs by **William Bartlett**

Printed in Canada
11 10 09 08 07   2 3 4 5 6

Publisher Cataloging-in-Publication Data

Bartlett, Therese.
    When you were born in Vietnam :
a memory book for children adopted
from Vietnam / written and designed by
Therese Bartlett ; with photographs by
William Bartlett.
-- 1st ed.
    p. cm.
    ISBN: 0-9638472-5-2

    1. Adoption--Vietnam. 2. Vietnam--
Description and travel. 3. Vietnam--
Pictorial works.   I. Bartlett, William,
1962- II. Title.

HV875.58.V54B37 2001   362.73'4'09597
                        QBI01-200811

When You Were Born in Vietnam
A Memory Book for Children Adopted From Vietnam

ISBN-10: 0963847252
ISBN-13: 9780963847256
Text © 2001 by Therese Bartlett
Photos © 2001 by William Bartlett
All Rights Reserved.
Yeong & Yeong Book Company
1368 Michelle Drive
St. Paul, Minnesota 55123-1459
www.yeongandyeong.com

Acknowledgments:

The author and photographer thank Brian Boyd and Scott and Caroline Ticarro-Parker for providing the opportunity to work on this project, and for trusting us to keep our focus while also adopting our second child.

We sincerely thank our good friends in Vietnam and all the orphanage directors and nannies for their assistance, patience and friendship. Without their help, this book could not have been produced. *Cam on!*

We appreciate the time and talents of Ruthmarie Mitsch, Michael Wilt, and all those whose comments and suggestions on the manuscript challenged us to produce a better book. We are honored to have worked with you and thank you for your valuable input.

We are grateful to the families who generously allowed us to photograph their adoption experiences both at home and abroad. Thank you for letting us share your joy.

Our thanks to Maureen Convey and John Gappa, whose great care and love for our children is treasured.

And thanks to Mary Maguire, who willingly takes the helm each time our hearts are called back to Vietnam. Your assistance is appreciated more than you can know.

Proceeds from the sale of this book will be donated to Catalyst Foundation, a non-profit, non-political organization whose aim is to improve the lives of orphaned and abandoned Vietnamese children through adoption advocacy, child sponsorships and direct relief efforts so that the children may reach their full potential. For more information, please see page 44 or visit their website at **www.catalystfoundation.org.**

To our children, Moya and Nathan,
for bringing us to Vietnam in the first place.
You fill our world with joy.

ike all children, you have a special story that is different from all others. It is the story of your family.

Millions of children all over the world joined their families through adoption. Some of their stories begin in lands far away from their homes today. Your life begins in Vietnam, and maybe you wonder about the country you are from and what your life was like before you were welcomed into your new, forever family.

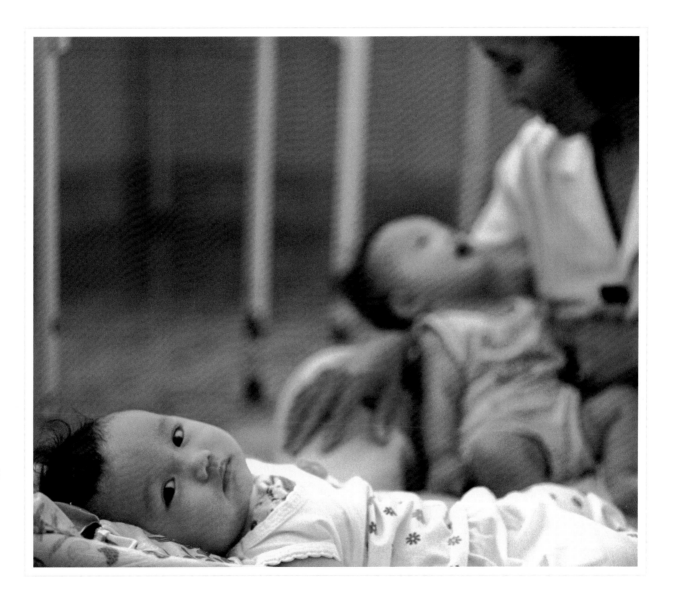

When you were born in Vietnam, many people touched your life. They cared for you and gave you everything you needed. They helped find a loving family for you. You were probably too small then to remember them now, but they played a very important role in your life. They still think about you today.

Vietnam is an ancient country. The people celebrate many of the same holidays and traditions their ancestors did years and years ago.

Vietnam is a beautiful land with majestic mountains, rich river beds and land for farming. Much has changed in Vietnam, but in many ways it is the same as it has been for thousands of years.

Today many people in Vietnam continue to work on the land, with some earning their living as rice farmers. Little boys called *thằng bé chăn trâu* tend to the water buffalo that help them plow their fields. Sometimes families raise their own ducks for eggs and meat. Or they fish the abundant waters of the South China Sea.

Some Vietnamese people live and work on small boats on rivers. Some live in small villages near places like the Mekong River Delta.

Others live in simple huts and work in the countryside where life is quiet and slow. They earn their living by making coconut candy or rice paper *(bánh tráng)* or colorful incense sticks, which they sell in the market.

Vietnam has big cities, too, such as Ho Chi Minh City and Hanoi. Many people live and work in the cities.

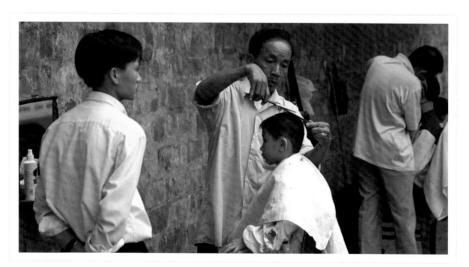

The smell of diesel fuel and the beeping of motorbike horns fill the air as people weave their way to the markets, work or school.

On nearly every street corner women sell piping hot *phở*, the traditional soup, or *bánh mì thịt*, delicious meat sandwiches. The markets sell just about anything anyone would ever need — clothing, fresh fruit, chickens and pigs, beautiful flowers and freshly baked breads.

Even with so much to offer, life in Vietnam can be a struggle. Houses are very expensive, and many families cannot afford one. They have no choice but to live in the streets or build small shacks on the edge of town.

Many young children cannot go to school. Instead they must work to buy food and to help support their families. Sometimes, no matter how much they try, people just can't earn enough money to take care of themselves and their family members.

You may have been born into a family that was already struggling to survive. Your birthparents knew that raising children is a serious responsibility. Because they loved you, they wanted to give you everything you needed in life. Perhaps they cared for you as best they could until they realized they could not provide you with all that a young child needs.

It is also possible that one of your birthparents became very ill, or died, or had to leave the other parent to care for you alone. Or maybe you needed medical help they could not afford.

Perhaps your birthmother was not married. In many places around the world, a woman who has a baby when she is unmarried does not receive any help from her family or community. She would have a very hard time working to earn a living and taking care of you at the same time.

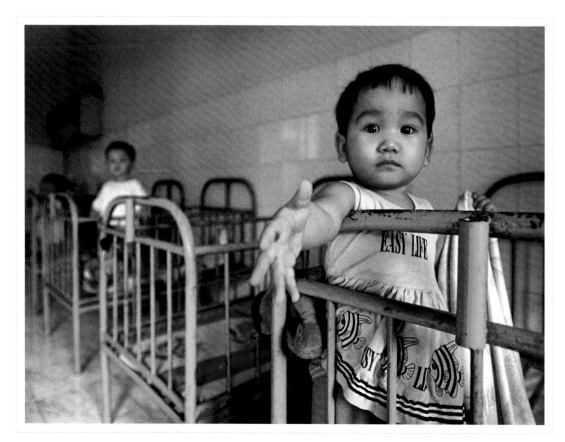

There may be other reasons your birthparents could not care for you in their family. The most important thing —
no matter what the reason — is that they wanted the best for you and your future. They learned that adoption is a way
to give a child a loving family that can care for the child's needs. Adoption seemed like the best plan for them.

Your birthmother may have asked for help figuring out who would take care of you. Social workers probably made the arrangements needed for your care after your birth. Or, if she didn't know about getting help from a social worker, your birthmother might have quietly slipped away from the hospital after you were born. She knew that you would be safe there, and that the hospital staff would know how to make plans for your care.

No matter what happened, saying goodbye was probably one of the hardest things she ever had to do. Her wish for you was that you have a good life.

As a little baby, maybe you needed to stay in the hospital for extra medical care. But as soon as you were ready, you were probably taken to an orphanage.

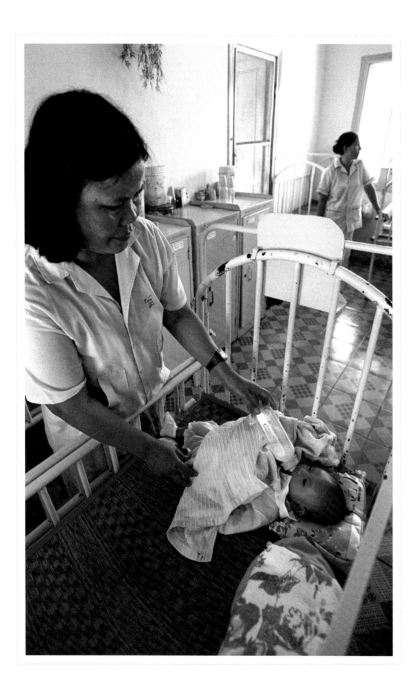

An orphanage is a place you go to live when there is no one else to care for you.

The orphanage was a busy place. Nannies *(bảo mẫu)* moved all around, taking care of many little babies — feeding them, changing their diapers and giving them baths.

Sometimes the nannies just held the babies. Babies need to be held and cuddled and played with a lot. Some orphanages don't have enough workers to watch over so many children, but they do the best they can to care for them all. Sadly, some children might never be adopted, and they remain at the orphanage to help care for the younger children.

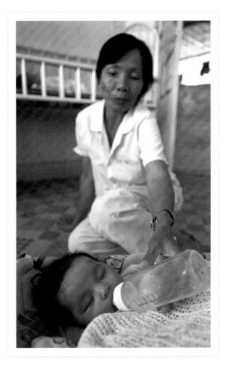

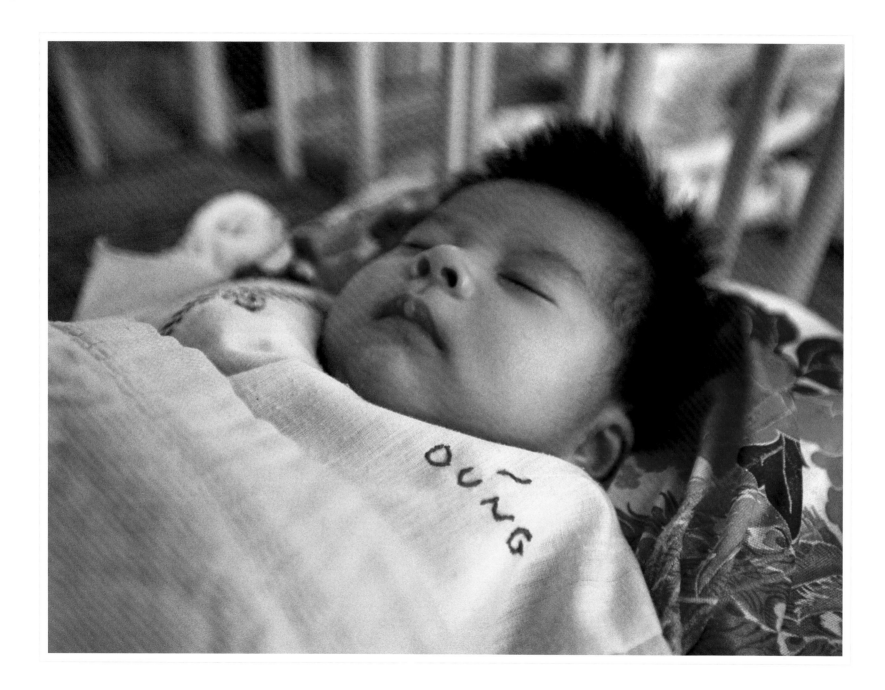

You had a crib to sleep in. It was marked with your name and had a reed mat *(chiếu)* on the bottom. It was covered with a net to keep the mosquitoes away from you. That's where you took your naps and got the sleep you needed to grow up big and strong.

While you were sleeping, the nannies tended to the needs of the other children, all the while keeping a watchful eye over you in case you awakened or cried out.

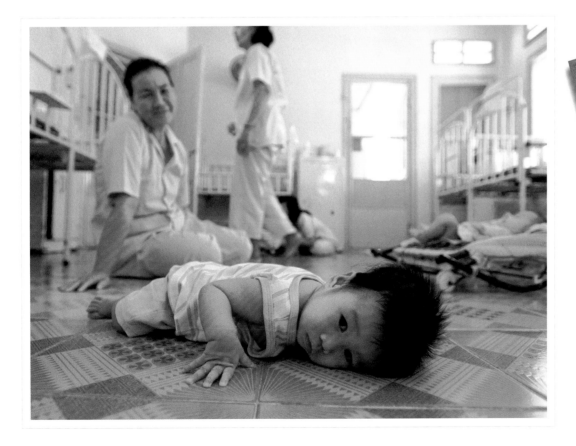

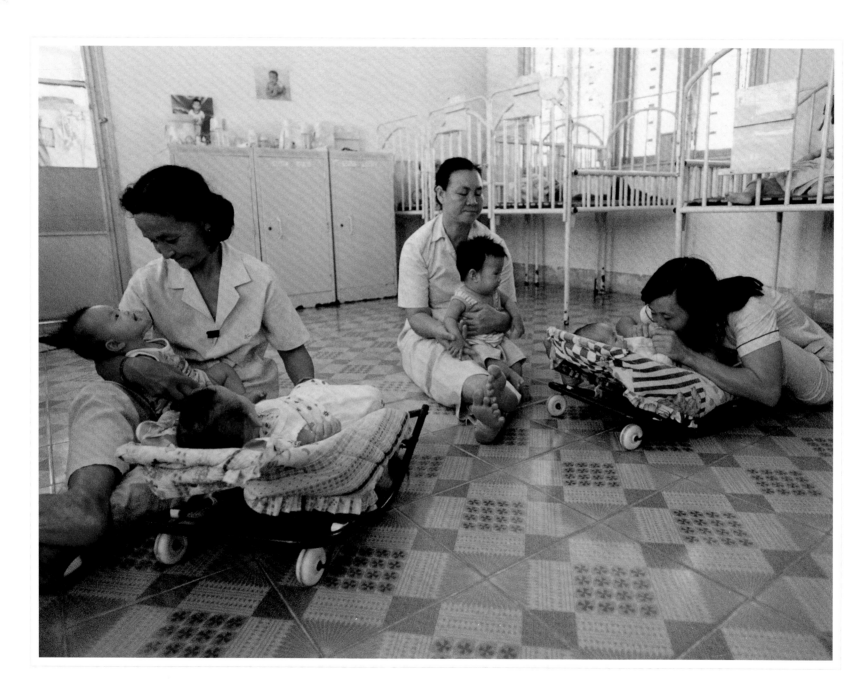

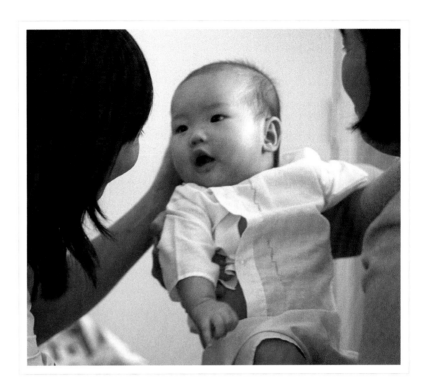

The nannies probably gave you your name,
which may have described where you were born
or what you were wearing the first time they saw
you. They would coo at you and laugh with you.
They sat on the floor and played games with you.
They would comfort you gently when you were
scared or sad.

They sang soft lullabies to you as you fell asleep in
their arms. You, and all the children, were well
cared for by these loving women.

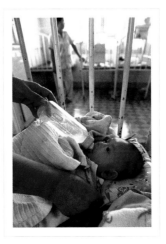

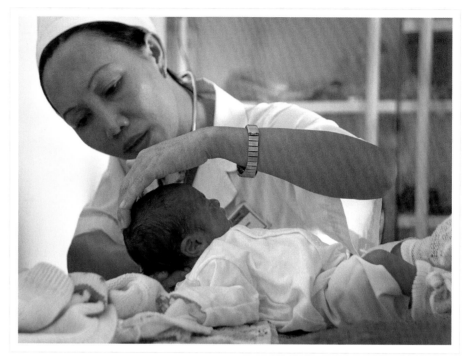

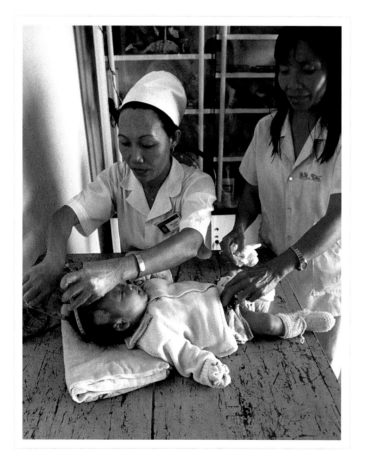

Every few weeks a doctor came to examine all the children at the orphanage. The doctor would measure how tall you were and how much you weighed. If any of you were sick, the doctor gave you medicine to make you feel better. The nannies listened to the doctor's instructions and made sure you were cared for properly. They might have taken your picture to show how much you had grown. They took pride in keeping you happy and healthy.

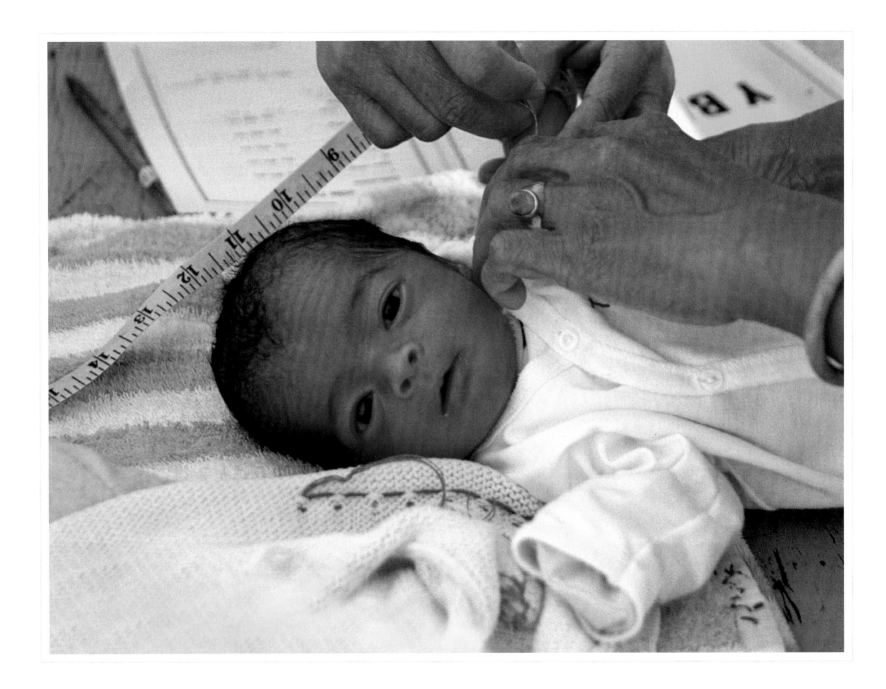

At about the same time you arrived at the orphanage, the people who ran it began to search for a new family for you. Your picture and the notes the doctor had made about you were sent to the Vietnamese officials in charge of adoptions.

Somewhere else — in Vietnam or in another country — was a family who wanted more than anything to love and raise a special child like you. That family contacted an adoption agency and asked for help in finding a boy or girl who needed a family. They filled out many papers and wrote a letter asking the officials in Vietnam to please consider placing a child in their home.

One day, your new family received the news they had been waiting for — a child needed them very much, and was waiting for them, too. They were so happy! It was such a special day!

Not long after that, your new family received a packet of information from the adoption agency. It contained some medical information about you and one or maybe several photos of you. Finally, after so much waiting, they could see the child they had dreamed of for so long! They wanted to pack their suitcases and come to be with you right away. Oh, how they longed to kiss you and hold you in their arms!

But your new family had to wait several weeks, or even several months, to meet you in person. It was hard for them to continue waiting, especially now that they had your picture and were growing so attached to you. You had already found a special place in their hearts.

While they waited, they kept busy by getting ready for your arrival. They prepared your room and bought clothing and toys for you. It was a very special time of waiting for everyone!

Then one day your new family was told that you were ready to be brought home. *Your* family. *Your* home. They packed up everything they needed to care for you on the trip. Babies and toddlers need lots of stuff!

After a very long plane ride, your new parents arrived in Vietnam. They were tired, but could hardly wait to meet you in person.

Shortly after their arrival, your new family was probably taken to the orphanage to see you for the first time, and maybe even hold you in their arms. They were probably very nervous. They couldn't believe they were finally going to meet you face to face. They had waited so long. They walked up to the doors of the orphanage and went slowly inside.

And there you were!

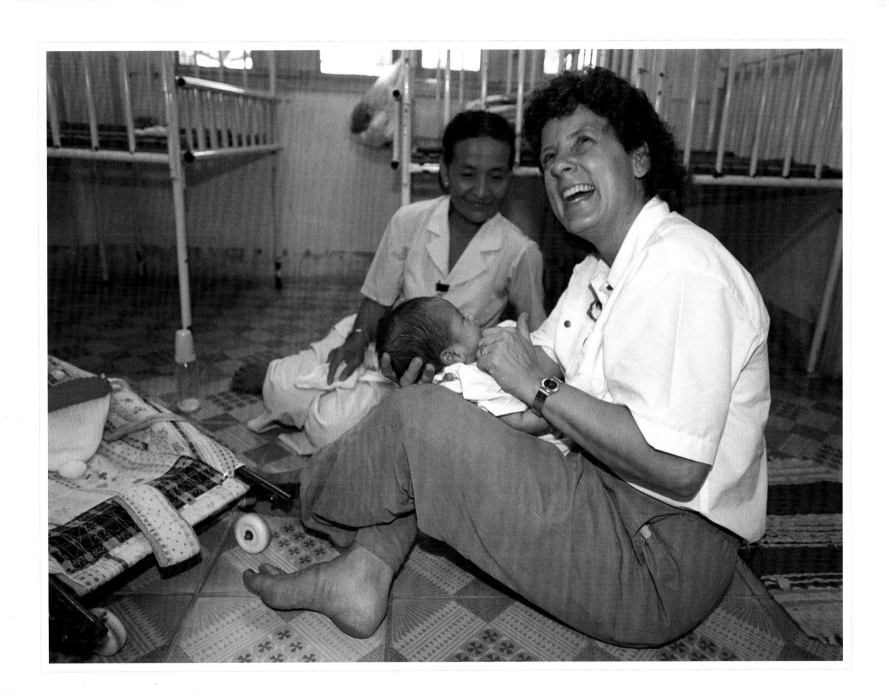

Everyone cried when your family held you closely for the first time. You may have cried, too, not knowing who they were, and feeling unsure why they were holding you so close. You didn't recognize their faces or how they smelled or even the language they spoke, yet they seemed to care for you a great deal. They whispered sweet-sounding words to you, and you enjoyed all the attention.

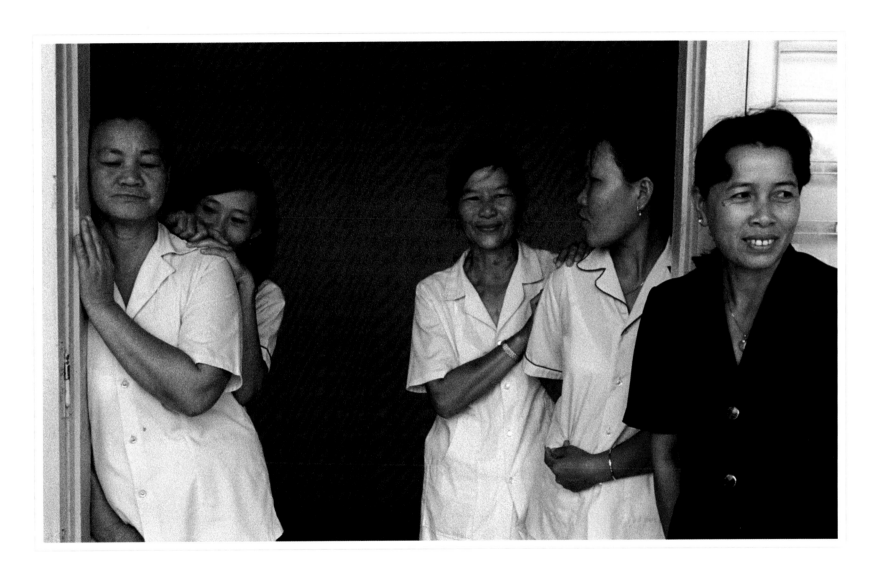

The nannies were excited, too, but also a little sad. They knew that they would soon have to say goodbye to you, and they would miss you. But they were also very happy, knowing that you would soon be going home with your new family.

One day not long after you met your new family, you were dressed in special clothing for a really big event to celebrate the beginning of your lives together. They took you to a very important meeting with the officials who had worked so hard to find a new home for you. This was your Giving and Receiving Ceremony.

Everyone was nervous and excited as they entered the government center. Your new parents and the officials signed many papers and your parents promised to send pictures of you as you grow up, and information about your health, to the officials in Vietnam. They also promised to help you learn about and understand your Vietnamese culture, because your birth country has given you a great heritage, and you can be proud of it.

They might have made a speech about how important you are to them. When the Giving and Receiving Ceremony was over, everyone knew your family would do their very best to love you, teach you, and care for you all your life.

Now you were officially welcomed into your new family. Everyone celebrated and thanked one another.

What a very happy day!

After the ceremony, you stayed with your new family while they finished the adoption process in Vietnam. They gave you toys to play with and clothes to wear. One of the nannies from the orphanage may have joined your family to help care for you. How nice for your new family to learn all about you from someone who had cared for you before them. And what special memories they will be able to share with you when you are older!

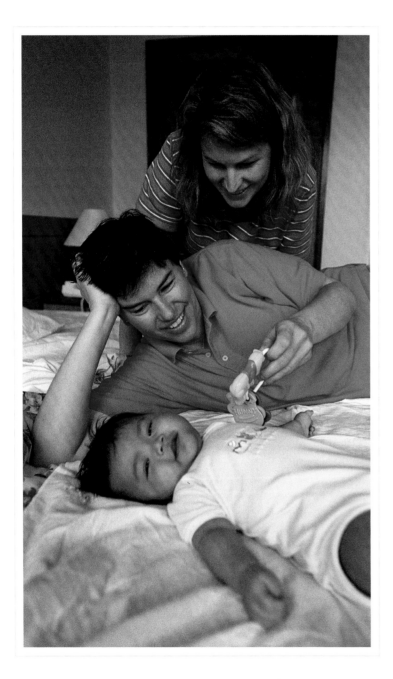

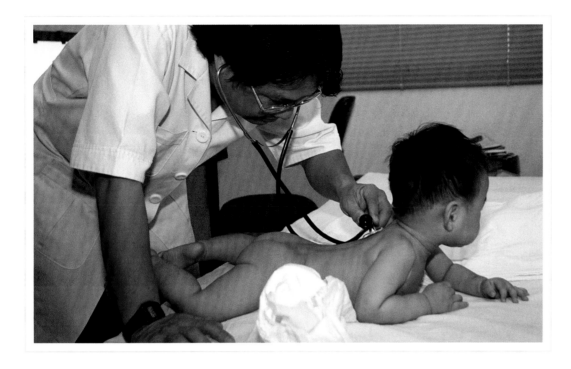

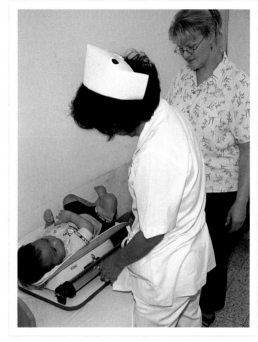

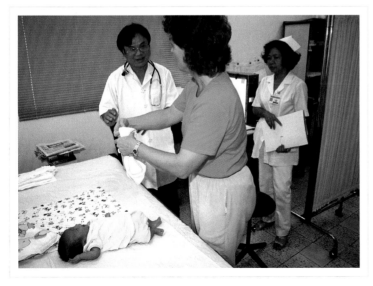

During these days you took a special trip with your mom or dad to the hospital, where the doctors made sure you were in good health and able to travel to your new home. They also met with government officials who reviewed your adoption paperwork. Then you had your picture taken for your travel visa and passport.

You and your family probably went out to learn more about Vietnam and to see the beautiful country in which you were born.

Finally, the day came when all the paperwork was done and your family could take you home. It was hard to say goodbye to all the new friends they had made in Vietnam, to all who had cared for you and loved you so much.

The airport was busy and noisy, and all the excitement was confusing. But soon you settled in for your long airplane ride home.

Excited family and friends gathered to wait for your arrival.
As they watched for your plane to land, they got ready to
greet you with colorful signs and balloons.

Finally, you came off the plane with your family. You met new friends and family members. Cameras flashed, people cried happy tears, and there was a lot of joyful noise. You were welcomed home.

Home at last!

It was such a long journey to your new family! Many wonderful people helped you along the way. Your birthparents in Vietnam, especially your birthmother, gave you your start and chose a new life for you. The nannies, doctors, social workers and officials did their best to keep you healthy and helped find the family that would be the one for you. They all played important parts in your life.

You are forever in their hearts.

May you keep them in your heart as you grow.

About the author and photographer:

Therese Bartlett worked in the field of graphic design for more than 25 years. In 2005 she joined Lutheran Social Service of Minnesota (www.minnesotaadoption.org) to help develop their Vietnam Adoption Program, where she works with Catalyst Foundation to facilitate adoptions from Vietnam. She is delighted to now focus her career on helping families through their own adoption journeys.

William Bartlett is a commercial photographer with more than 25 years experience in advertising and editorial photography. He has produced award-winning work for major corporations and has received top honors and recognition for his personal work. Nothing has been so rewarding as his experiences while photographing the people of Vietnam.

Together they are the proud parents of two children adopted from Vietnam. The Bartletts are active members in the local FCVN Chapter (Vietnam Midwest Danh Tu). They founded Little Red Fairy's *My Vietnam* art contests which help impoverished Vietnamese children earn scholarships while building pride in their culture and individual accomplishments. The children have responded by the thousands with revealing and inspiring art. The Bartletts look forward to their next opportunity to make that long trip across the ocean to see their cherished new friends and family in Vietnam.

For further information and support:

Catalyst Foundation
Catalyst Foundation is a non-profit, non-political organization whose aim is to improve the lives of Vietnamese children so that they may reach their full potential. Founded by parents of twin girls adopted from Vietnam in 1998, Catalyst Foundation works diligently to make positive change for the children of Vietnam. Foundation projects include adoption advocacy, direct relief, Aid Expeditions, and their life-changing Child Sponsorship Program which empowers provincial leaders to deliver health services, food, clothing and educational assistance to children in need. Catalyst Foundation also organizes the Vietnam Culture Camps (held annually in Minnesota and on the east coast) where Vietnamese adoptees and their families take time to celebrate with old and new friends while sharing and learning about their Vietnamese heritage. Proceeds from the sale of this book will support these activities. **www.catalystfoundation.org**.

AdoptVietnam
AdoptVietnam is a website devoted to the promise, practice and parenting realities of adoption from Vietnam. It is an in-depth guide to resources and information on travel to Vietnam, Vietnamese culture and adoption from Vietnam whose goal is to be the most comprehensive online guide to adoption from that beautiful and vibrant nation. AdoptVietnam.org is not affiliated with any agency, facilitator, institution or government. It is supported by the efforts, inspiration and energy of adoptive and prospective adoptive families across the world. **www.adoptvietnam.org**.

Families with Children from Vietnam
FCVN is the national organization of families who have adopted or are waiting to adopt children from Vietnam. Their website provides a meeting place where adoptive families share photographs of their children, personal adoption stories, adoption status and more. Their website also includes FCVN chapter listings, local FCVN announcements and support for new chapters. **www.fcvn.org**.

Photo index and annotations:

The photographs in this book were taken in December 2000 and January 2001, in and around the cities of Hanoi, Hue, Phan Thiet, Ho Chi Minh City, and the Mekong Delta. For a more detailed listing of the subject matter and locations, please check our website at www.yeongandyeong.com.

All photographs © William Bartlett, except page 32 (courtesy of John Gappa) and pages 26-27 (referral photos, courtesy of CHSM-VNP).

Additional copies of *When You Were Born in Vietnam* can be ordered from adoption specialty mail order catalogs, from Catalyst Foundation, or directly from Yeong & Yeong Book Company.

Other titles in this series: *When You Were Born in China* and *When You Were Born in Korea*.

Also published by Yeong & Yeong Book Company: *A Passage to the Heart*, writings from families with children from China, *I Wish for You a Beautiful Life*, letters from the Korean birthmothers of Ae Ran Won to their children, and *Voices from Another Place*, a collection of works from a generation born in Korea and adopted to other countries.

Yeong & Yeong supports charitable fund-raising. Discounts are available on quantity purchases by support groups and adoption agencies who would like to use any of these books as a fund-raiser.

To place an order or for more information, please contact:

Yeong & Yeong Book Company
1368 Michelle Drive
St. Paul, Minnesota 55123-1459
www.yeongandyeong.com

Brian Boyd, Publisher
bboyd@yeongandyeong.com